ST AGNES

A PHOTOGRAPHIC HISTORY

VOLUME IV

UP GOONOWN & GOONBELL

CLIVE BENNEY

WHEAL HAWKE
PUBLICATIONS

FOREWORD

This book, the fourth in a series about St Agnes, starts at Rosemundy (where the previous volume ended) and will take the reader on a trip from Rosemundy up Goonown to Goonbell. A thousand years ago St Agnes was distinctive for its great tracts of heathland, surrounding scattered islands of fields and habitations. Today it is only along the coast and on the Beacon that the ancient heath survives. Place-names give a hint of this vanished downland – Goonown, Goonbell, Goonlaze, Gooninnis (Goon = downland). With the increase in mining during the 18th and 19th centuries St Agnes steadily grew, and small hamlets at Goonown and Goonbell appeared. The ancient heathland was enclosed and broken up into miners' smallholdings, a cottage with a few acres of small fields. Each little hamlet had it own identity with much rivalry between them. Early maps show two distinct areas, though today it's hard to tell where Goonown ends and Goonbell begins. In the book you will see that Goonown and Goonbell were once self-sufficient with shops, cobbler, post office and chapels, but sadly these have all gone and a trip into St Agnes or even Truro is required to get the everyday essentials.

I have continued to extract information from old newspapers, trade directories and other historical documents, but as before I have also relied on oral history from the numerous people I have visited.

Clive Benney, 2012

First published in 2012 by
Wheal Hawke Publications:

14 Trevaunance Road, St Agnes,
Cornwall, TR5 0SE

Design by Daniel Benney
www.danielbenney.co.uk

ISBN 978-0-9550510-4-3

Printed by R Booth Ltd:

The Praze, Penryn,
Cornwall, TR10 8AA

CONTENTS

The New Connexion Chapel and Masonic Hall...........................8

Rosemundy 14

Rosemundy House 18

Up Goonown 22

The Lawrences of Goonown 28

John Lawry's Carpenter's Shop and The St John Ambulance Hall 32

Ste Harris, Goonown 42

Goonown Chapel 44

Goonown Football Club 62

Goonown Playing Field 64

Goonown and The Greeny 72

Goonbell 76

Goonbell Chapel 88

Goonbell Football Club 94

Ropewalk 98

Goonbell Halt 100

References 104

Acknowledgements 106

The remains of four thatched cottages in Water Lane, St Agnes, destroyed by fire on the 14th May 1909. Behind on the skyline is Gooninnis engine house and headgear. The engine house contained a 50 inch Cornish beam engine that had previously worked at Trevaunance and Penhalls mine.

THE
NEW CONNEXION CHAPEL
& MASONIC HALL

Today in Rosemundy stands a large building known as the Masonic Hall. It has two floors, the Trevaunance Masonic Lodge Temple and ante-room above and a hall below. The building was erected in 1835 as a chapel for the Methodist New Connexion, following some difference with the Wesleyan Methodists at Goonown. (The New Connexion joined other groups to form the United Methodist Church in 1907.) The *Book of St Agnes: Descriptive Official Guide* of 1925 states: 'The late General William Booth, founder of the Salvation Army, preached here before that world-wide organisation was started [i.e. before 1865].'

The chapel held regular Tea Treats in the field adjoining. When they had their tea in July 1923 they probably did not realise that it was to be one of their last. The *Royal Cornwall Gazette* newspaper reported: 'The scholars of the United Methodist Sunday School held their annual tea on Saturday. Fine weather and the presence of St Agnes Town Band brought together a large number in the evening.' Within two years the chapel was closed and sold due to lack of support. On the 17th June 1925 the following appeared in the *Royal Cornwall Gazette*: 'The trustees of the old Methodist New Connection [sic] chapel have sold the chapel by auction for £240.'

c. 1900: members of the New Connexion chapel outside the front door.

New Connexion tea in 1907 in the field where the old British Legion Hall now stands.

A large number of children and adults at the New Connexion (United Methodist) tea in 1911. The field behind is now part of Castle Meadows.

The chapel had been purchased by the St Agnes Masonic Lodge, Trevaunance No. 4668. In *A History of Trevaunance Lodge of Free and Accepted Masons No. 4668, 1925-1975* we read:

> For many years before 1924 there had been a number of Freemasons resident in St Agnes who were, in the main, members of Boscawen Lodge No. 699 at Chacewater. Those members were instrumental in inducing that Lodge, which was warranted in 1857, to sponsor the formation of Trevaunance as a Daughter Lodge. After much preliminary work the new Lodge was granted its Warrant on the 6th August, 1924. There followed a great deal more detailed arrangements in preparation for the Consecration which was held in St. Mary's Wesleyan Hall, Truro, on April 2nd, 1925.

From April 1925 until November of that year the Lodge met in the Church Hall, but it was realised from the outset that this building was far from ideal, and clearly arrangements were already in hand for the acquisition of the old chapel.

In September the following resolution was carried in open Lodge: 'That this Lodge having purchased a building at Rosemundy, now known as Trevaunance Hall and previously known as the United Methodist Chapel, request permission from the Most Worshipful Grand Master to hold all future meetings in this Hall, it being the opinion of this Lodge that in every way the new premises are more suitable, and being our own property, can be most adequately adapted for the purpose of the Lodge business.' Copies of the resolution were sent to the Grand Secretary and the Provincial Grand Secretary. By the November meeting the Dispensation had arrived, and also a letter from the Provincial Grand Secretary congratulating the Lodge on having obtained permanent quarters.

The first Lodge meeting in the new premises was on Tuesday the 8th December 1925. By this time, work in adapting the building to its new use had advanced sufficiently to enable the Lodge to assemble in the large room on the ground floor.

In late 1933 work commenced on the building of a new Temple on the first floor, together with an ante-room and a staircase to give access. This new Lodge Temple was formally opened on the 13th March 1934. With the building of the new first floor, the ground floor hall became available for dances and other functions and could be hired from the Lodge.

In September 1941 the Lodge arranged terms with the County Education Authority for the use of the upstairs ante-room as a classroom for evacuated children. The room was used as a schoolroom for several months, but the toilet and recreational facilities were so limited that the premises were de-requisitioned at the first opportunity.

During the Second World War, with the anti-aircraft practice camp at St Agnes Head and Trevellas Airfield in the immediate vicinity, the adult population increased tremendously. Apart from the small Regal Cinema, recreational facilities in the village were nil, so it was not surprising that the downstairs hall, which had previously been little used by the public, was in great

...the hall became a 'Palais De Danse for the troops'

demand. In 1940 it was leased to Mr Tremearne at £20 a year and he had sole use except when it was required by the Lodge. From then onwards, as it says in *The History of Trevaunance Lodge*, the hall became a 'Palais De Danse for the troops' and much money was raised for charities.

From the war to the present day, apart from minor alterations inside, the building has changed very little. The upstairs still remains the Trevaunance Lodge Temple and ante-room with the hall below.

A view towards the New Connexion (United Methodist) chapel c. 1912.

The building in 2008 with the Trevaunance Lodge Temple upstairs and hall below.

ROSEMUNDY

Peter Thomas, in the *Journal of the St Agnes Museum Trust, no. 2* derives the name Rosemundy from Cornish '*ros* (promontory; hill-spur, moor, high ground) + *mon-dy* (mineral house) = hillside with a mineral house'. Place-name expert Oliver Padel, in an interview with Ted Gundry for the radio series *Village of the Week* in 1987, preferred one of the other meanings of 'ros' for his definition, saying that it was an Old Cornish word meaning much the same as 'goon' (downland) and that 'mon-dy' meant 'mine house', so 'downs of the mine house'.

Butcher Ste Harris sharpens his knife beside his horse-drawn butcher's wagon on the road near the Masonic Hall in 1906.

James (Jimmy) Thomas on his greengrocery round at
Rosemundy in the 1930s. He stored his produce in a
shed/garage at Goonbell and covered the St Agnes area.
A tarpaulin was carried to protect his goods in wet weather.

ros (promontory; hill-spur, moor,
high ground) + *mon-dy* (mineral house)
= hillside with a mineral house.

Rosemundy showing Tinten (right) c. 1910.

It is believed that the house now called Tinten dates back to the 1840s, although a building appears on this site on the 1813 Ordnance Survey map. It has often been said that the property had a connection with Captain William Bligh, of the *Bounty* fame. He was born at Tinten Manor, St Tudy, on the 9th September 1754. Previous occupants of the house have even said that Bligh had the house built and stayed there. A raised walkway at the rear of the building is known as 'The Captain's Walkway', where Bligh is alleged to have walked up and down. The answer however comes from Colin Harris, grandson of Hannah Harris, née Blight, who owned the house and ran the school. Hannah's research showed that she was a distant relative of William Bligh's sister. Because of this link she named the house Tinten. William Bligh himself, it would appear, had no connection with the house.

Old maps show a 'Pound' on the Goonown side of Tinten. This is where stray animals were taken and kept until owners paid a fee for their return.

This old postcard is postmarked 1904 and shows children posing for the photographer in Rosemundy. The children stand outside their school, which adjoined the house called Tinten. Mrs Hannah Harris paid £200 for the house in the 1880s and the school-room was later added on the side. Trade directories show that she taught here up to the First World War.

Hannah Harris, centre, sits with her pupils in the grounds of Tinten c. 1905.

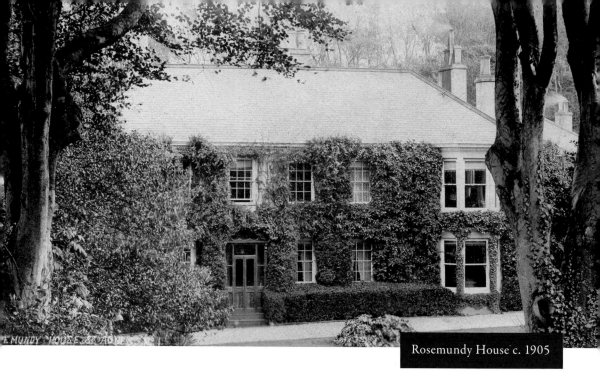

ROSEMUNDY HOUSE

Research suggests that Rosemundy House dates back to about 1780, with perhaps some older portions. The surrounding land was part of the Donnithorne estate before being sold to John James, who built the house. He also acquired a considerable amount of other land in the St Agnes and Mingoose area. After his death the house was purchased by Thomas Humphries and later passed to his son Henry Humphries, a mine purser. Around 1840 it became the property of William Carne. William came from Falmouth where his family was involved in shipping and importing as well as banking and wine and general trade. In 1851 William moved back to Falmouth, and for the next fifteen years the house was occupied by George Hugoe. He was employed by the Carne family as a clerk. The next owner of the house was William Naylor Carne, who was a nephew to the first William Carne and had inherited the property from his uncle, taking possession in 1865. He was also involved in the family business at Falmouth. Many beautiful trees and shrubs were planted in the grounds by William Naylor Carne, who was a pioneer in the cultivation of narcissi. He died in 1906, and the house was sold to Francis Newberry Adkin, a retired tobacco manufacturer from Bromley in Kent. It is not clear how much time he spent at Rosemundy as in the 1911 census he is shown as living in Kent, and Rosemundy House is occupied by Thomas Collins, a caretaker/carpenter also born in Bromley. In 1919 Mr Adkin sold the property to three ladies: Lady Mary Trefusis, Lady Catherine Seward Hain and Frances Jane Bolitho. These ladies turned the house into the Cornwall County Mother and Baby Home. Mothers came from all over the South West of England to have their babies here, and during the next 45 years approximately 1200 babies were born at the home. Following the birth of their babies, mothers would remain at the home for another nine months to learn how to look after them, and also domestic skills like cooking and sewing, not only for their babies but for possible employment on leaving the home. Later, after the War, the mothers would stay for a much shorter time, usually just eight weeks after giving birth, when the babies either left with them or were placed for adoption. By 1960 the building had become too large for Cornwall's needs and the expense of maintaining it became too great, leading to its eventual closure in 1964.

The house then remained empty for a while, before being purchased by Mr Derek Tabor. He converted the building into a hotel, which opened in 1967. It remains a hotel today.

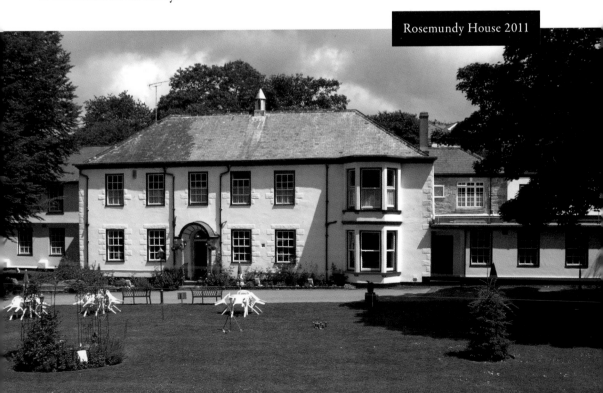

Rosemundy House 2011

Babies in cots outside Rosemundy House c. 1922

UP GOONOWN

Most of the outlying districts and villages around St Agnes have a preposition attached to them when they are referred to by people of St Agnes village. 'Down Quay', 'Over Mingoose' and 'Up Goonown' are three examples of this habit.

Cornish scholar J.E.B. Gover in his *Place-Names of Cornwall*, held at the Courtney Library, Truro, states that in the Henderson manuscripts Goonown is shown in 1612 as 'Gooneowne'. Peter Thomas, in the *Journal of the St Agnes Museum Trust, no. 2* (having already defined 'goon' as 'downland'), writes: 'Goonown. *goon* + ? At least two explanations of the second element have been advanced, *guyn* (white) and *oghan* (oxen), but neither is confirmed so far by early forms of the name.' Oliver Padel, in his interview with Ted Gundry in the *Village of the Week* radio series, put forward another possibility: "'Goon' is the Cornish word for 'downland', 'open grazing', and a large part of St Agnes parish must have been open grazing formerly so we get ... Goonown, which literally seems to mean 'the downs of fear', 'the fearful downs', although I don't know why they should be so called.'

Two ladies having a ride in Ralph Butson's jingle at Goonown in the 1960s. Ralph stands beside his horse Queenie, who for many years pulled the jingle. Ralph bottled and delivered his own milk from his farm at Goonown to various parts of St Agnes. The milk churn was in the middle, with the crates on the side. Ralph stopped delivering in the late 1960s and his family say he was the last person in St Agnes to deliver goods using a horse. Goonown Farmhouse, where Ralph lived, is one of the oldest buildings in Goonown, and the Butson family have lived here for at least seven generations.

Goonown c. 1905

In this picture of Goonown the man on the left wearing the white apron and jacket is John Lawry, the carpenter and undertaker, his premises being a little further up the road near where the photographer is standing to take this picture. On the right is another man dressed similarly, who was probably employed by John Lawry. Each man keeps a child very still while the picture is taken.

Just to the right of centre is a small building with a chimney, that butts up to the road. Today it has the appearance of a small chapel, but no record of this use has been found. A clue to its possible early use, however, can be found in the notes of Maurice Bizley, held in the County Museum at Truro. These notes were compiled in the early 1950s, most, but not all, used in his book *Friendly Retreat*. At this time he interviewed older residents of Goonown, including Victor Trezise, then in his eighties. One portion reads: 'Next door to Lawrence Villas is a small low building. Half a century ago was a bakery run by Mr Sanders.' Jane Adams bought the property in 1983, and at that time an old gent stopped and said he remembered going to the building to collect bread when he was a child. The man's identity is not known.

Goonown stores c. 1940, run by Arthur Keast and his wife. They took over the shop in the mid 1930s from Mary Ann Mitchell, who appears here in trade directories as far back as 1914. It seems likely however that it was a shop long before this. Around 1950 Cecil and Muriel Tremain took over the business, and it remained a shop under different owners until the 1970s when it was converted into a dwelling, number 73 Goonown.

Muriel Tremain outside Goonown Stores in the 1950s.

Elephants at Goonown in the early 1930s – they belonged to a circus performing in a field below the playing field at Goonown (the St Agnes side known as 'Tom Bennetts' Field'). Here they are being walked through Goonown down to the beach and back, and stopping to allow the locals to touch their trunks. Phyllis Robinson remembers the circus coming most years to Goonown. The field was also used by fairs when they came to the village.

THE LAWRENCES OF GOONOWN

In Goonown today can be seen a pair of semi-detached granite-fronted houses that bear the dates 1759 and 1894 high up on the front. They are numbered 11 and 12 Goonown and look very grand compared to the cottages nearby. Originally they were named 1 and 2 Lawrence Villas. The Lawrence family, it is believed, originally came from the north of England, but by the beginning of the eighteenth century Joseph Lawrence and his wife Alice lived at St Ives in Cornwall. The book *The Lawrences of Cornwall*, written in 1915, tells how Thomas, the son of Joseph and Alice, moved to St Agnes, where on the 16th April 1759 he married Jane Rowsse [sic]. During this year he built for himself a cottage at Goonown, hence the first date. In the book the cottage is described as 'A good sized thatched cottage of cobb [sic], to which, later, was added a wooden facing. The building was afterwards enlarged, and the house-part made high enough to enable a basket to be hung on the beam of the ceiling without touching the heads of those walking beneath.' This cottage was to become the birthplace of a distinguished line of Lawrences who were to hold office as Alderman and Lord Mayor of London and to become knights and baronets.

Thomas and Jane had a son, another Thomas. Born in 1760, he followed the trade of carpenter and, on the 1st April 1788, married Mary Tonkin of St Agnes. Thomas and Mary had eight sons and four daughters, the eldest of whom being William, born in St Agnes on the 4th February 1789. He also became a carpenter but in 1808, aged 19, 'left St Agnes with two guineas in his pocket and a bag of tools on his back, accompanied by two young friends employed in the same handicraft. They worked their way to Plymouth, and thence took a ship to London. Their first important piece of work in the great City was the making of square balusters for a staircase, for which they were each paid £5, accompanied with the offer of a second engagement on the same terms. Lawrence's two companions would take up no fresh work until they had disposed of the cash on hand; while he at once seized the further opportunity, and engaged a couple of men as his assistants.'

This was the beginning of his business career. He never looked back and built for himself a very successful building company. In 1819 he was made a Freeman of the City of London and in 1849 was chosen as Sheriff of London and Middlesex. He was deeply attached to the cause of education and was instrumental in the provision of new school-rooms for the British School in St Agnes, whose establishment he had encouraged. It was expressly made open to all without denominational restriction. The foundation stone of the new building was laid on the 2nd January 1837, on a site which he leased to the school authority, and the school was opened later in the same year.

In 1817 William had married Jane Clarke in London, by which time, back in St Agnes, both his grandparents had died, Jane Lawrence in the February and Thomas in the August of 1811. His own father, Thomas, had also died, aged 52, on the 13th March 1812. His mother, Mary Lawrence, survived her husband by over 38 years, dying at Goonown in April 1850. In 1855 William himself died, by which time he had become an Alderman as well as Sheriff of London and Middlesex.

Back in 1818, William and Jane had had a son, also William, the eldest of eleven, who later became a partner in his father's business. Like his father, he rose rapidly in civic ranks and by 1863 was Lord Mayor of London. In 1887 he was knighted by Queen Victoria. Sir William did not forget his father's birthplace, and in about 1872 the freehold of the site of the British School at St Agnes was conveyed by him to the school authorities. The thatched cottage in Goonown, built by his grandfather in 1759, still belonged to the family, but he considered it unsanitary, and so in 1894 he had it pulled down and had the two granite attached houses built that now bear the two dates.

Sir William Lawrence died a bachelor in 1897, and the family duties fell on his younger brother Edwin, born in 1837. Edwin was a very successful man in his own right and was elected MP for Truro in 1895. On the death of his elder brother the baronetcy passed to him, and in 1898 he received by royal licence the name of 'Durning Lawrence', taking the name of his wife Edith's family together with his own. Like his brother and father before him he did not forget St Agnes. He had a particular interest in the health care of people at large, and in 1894 he founded at his father's birthplace the St Agnes and District Nursing Association, contributing to its maintenance £50 a year from the first and, by deed of the 22nd October 1901, endowing it with two cottages and £1000 Plymouth Corporation Stock.

Number 11 became the home of the district nurse and number 12 was let. By 1935, twenty-one years after the death of Sir Edwin in 1914, the nurse had her own car thanks to the Durning-Lawrence Trust. Following the introduction of the National Health Service in 1948, however, the nurse and her car were removed.

The Durning-Lawrence Trust continues today, giving financial contributions to various local needy causes.

Thomas Lawrence's cottage, on the left, built in 1759.

Numbers 11 and 12 Goonown today.

JOHN LAWRY'S CARPENTER'S SHOP & THE ST JOHN AMBULANCE HALL

For over a hundred years a small building has stood in Goonown where the St Agnes Theatre Players' premises are today. This present building, however, is the second to occupy this site.

The first building to be erected here appears from old photographs to have been of wooden construction and was used by John Lawry for his builder's, carpenter's and undertaker's business. The structure is not shown on the 1880 Ordnance Survey map, but by the 1891 census John Lawry is shown living at Goonown. He is aged 23 years, the head of the family and an employer, and his occupation is given as a carpenter and undertaker.

John Lawry ran his business here for many years, and reference is made to him in the *St Agnes Police Occurrence Books*, held at the County Record Office, Truro, where it is stated that on the 10th May 1914 he gave P.C. Kitt 3/6d. (17½p) for assistance in conveying a body from Porthtowan beach to St Agnes. John Lawry was heavily involved in the Methodist Chapel at St Agnes, at first as a Sunday School pupil and later as a choir member and trustee. His distinctive face appears in many Tea Treat photographs.

Chapel records show that John died in 1917, and it appears that the wooden workshop was demolished after his death. The ground where it had stood became an open space until the late 1920s when it came up for sale by auction. The bidding was fierce between two local men but eventually Major Gilpin, of Goonown, was successful.

A group of people outside John Lawry's builder's and undertaker's shop c. 1906. John Lawry himself stands third from the right at the back. His name board, above the door, is dwarfed by an advertising board for Tom Moore's clothing shops.

Major Gilpin had the present building constructed around 1928. The part nearest the road he used as a garage and the rear was used by Albert Reynolds for his carpenter's, builder's and undertaker's business. It is interesting to note an entry on the first page of Albert Reynolds' account book for January 1927, under expenditure: 'Carpenters bench as per Miss E.G. Lawry 18/- [90p].' This suggests that he bought John Lawry's old bench from his daughter. Albert is shown as being here in the 1930 *Kelly's Trade Directory* and he stayed on for many years until he moved to new premises further up the road. After a few years, however, Major Gilpin's garage acquired a new use.

The St Agnes Division of the St John Ambulance Brigade was formed in early 1933. Its aim and purpose were to afford skilled assistance in cases of accident and sudden illness. The members were to take duty at football matches, other sports meetings and public gatherings; they were also to assist with the removal of patients by ambulance when necessary.

On the 12th April 1933 the *Royal Cornwall Gazette* reported as follows: 'Mr. W.W. Johnson, assistant County Commissioner of the St John Ambulance Association, presented certificates and vouchers to the members of the newly formed class at St Agnes on Wednesday. Dr. Whitworth was the lecturer (assisted by P.C. Mutton), and Dr. Pollock examined. Those receiving first-aid certificates were Messrs. W.J. Baker, J.S. Roscrow, S. Wills, J.F. Mitchell, G. Tatler, J.S. Repper, E.A. Wills, J.H. Solomon, W. Woolcock, H.R. Roberts, R. Luke, T. Smith; vouchers, J. Ferris and R. Wilson; labels, P.C. Mutton and R. Roberts.'

In January 1934 the newspaper reported that the Division under Ambulance Officer R.H. Wilson was passed as efficient by Assistant Commissioner Mr W.W. Johnson, and on the 25th April 1934 recorded the following recipients of first-aid certificates: Messrs J. King, G. Watters [sic], J.S. Parnell, J. Clissold, G. Dyer and W. Carveth. Mr J. King (Mithian) was the class secretary. A week later the same paper reported that the funds of the division had been helped by a dance in the Masonic Hall. Miss O. Vellanoweth was responsible for the arrangements and a masked band played for the dances. Mr Polkinhorn was the M.C.

When inspected in November 1934 by Lieut. Col. Blackwood DSO, the County Commissioner, the members were led by Ambulance Officer R. Weymouth Wilson (appointed to the rank of Superintendent), and the drill was conducted by Sgt R. Roberts and Corp. R. Luke. They were congratulated by the Commissioner on the excellence of their drill, their smart appearance and their discipline. The next lessons for them, said Col. Blackwood, would be in gas mask drill.

The following report appeared in the *St Agnes Parish Church Magazine* in January 1937:

> The St Agnes Division of the St John Ambulance Brigade was formed over three and a half years ago. The division has provided First-Aid boxes at the Quay, Peterville and Chapel Porth, which have proved to be very useful; they are replenished with dressings, bandages and other First-Aid materials from brigade funds. Since the formation of the Division First-Aid has been rendered in over 136 cases of accident. All members are annually re-examined (in First-Aid) by a Doctor and meet for practice on Wednesday night each week. This is necessary in order to remain an efficient unit. The Division is inspected each year by either the County Commissioner or the assistant County Commissioner. Lieutenant Colonel Blackwood, D.S.O., M.B., County Commissioner, was the inspecting officer this year. He congratulated the Division under Corporal R. Luke (officer in charge) on their smart appearance and also on the improvement made since the last visit. Although this was satisfactory, he said he would like to see an increased membership.

The *St Austell Gazette* newspaper of the 6th October 1937 carried the following report: 'St Agnes Ambulance Brigade at their annual meeting on Thursday evening welcomed the return of Sergt. R. Roberts to the active list, and elected him as officer in charge of the division. Corpl. R.H. Luke was elected as Hon. Secretary. The Hon. Treasurer (Mr E.W. Friston) reported a balance of £23 19s [£23.95]. It was decided to accept Mr Friston's offer of the Occupational

Cecil Tremain at the wheel of the Morris ambulance around 1940.

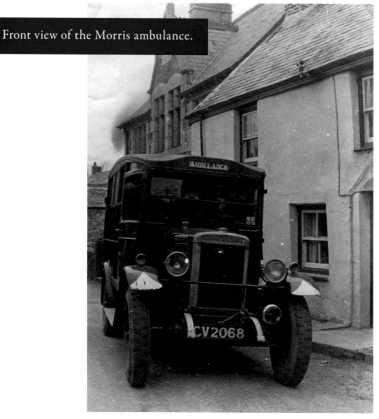

Front view of the Morris ambulance.

Centre Hall as headquarters. The Division proposes a course of lectures in first-aid, Dr W.C. Whitworth being the lecturer. All new members are cordially invited to attend.'

New members did join, and in March 1938 H.S. Williams, C.C. Tremain, R.E. Grigg, J.R. Millar, W.C. Grigg and F.A. Cheshire passed the first-aid examination and were enrolled as new members.

In May 1938 Dr W.C. Whitworth presided at the quarterly meeting held at the Goonown headquarters. It was announced that an agreement had been reached with Major Gilpin to rent the building as headquarters and that the major was being approached with a view to purchasing the freehold for the brigade. The question of the acquisition of a motor ambulance for the division at an early stage was discussed. The treasurer reported a balance in hand after all accounts were paid and nearly £10 in a separate building account. Suggestions were made for raising funds for the new ambulance.

In October a series of ten dances in the Masonic Hall began to raise funds for the ambulance. The music was provided by Fowey Fireside Fusiliers Radio Dance Band. At Christmas 1938 a Gala Dance was held in the hall. One hundred and twenty guests attended. Mr W.J. Martin was the M.C. and the band from Fowey again supplied the music. Novelty dance prizes were awarded to Miss L.V. Beck, Miss J. Barkle, Mr Horton Davey, Miss M. Roberts, Mr D. Chudleigh and Miss M. Bending. The best dressed ladies were Miss D. Keast, Miss S. Tremearne and Miss B. Trotter.

Eventually an ambulance was bought, a Morris Commercial. Cecil Tremain, Bill Woolcock and later Douglas Mitchell became the drivers. The ambulance was called to attend accidents and collapses and to convey bodies to the mortuary. Douglas Mitchell of Goonown, an ex-St John member, remembers using this ambulance to take bodies to the old mortuary in Vicarage Road, now the lychgate at the entrance to the garden of rest.

Donald Blight joined the St John Ambulance as a cadet in about 1938. He remembers the building at Goonown in three sections, the ambulance garage nearest the road, the lecture room, and a workshop, used by local builder Albert Reynolds, at the far end. When Albert Reynolds moved to a new workshop further up the road the Brigade had the whole building.

John King stands beside the new Vauxhall ambulance on the 11th May 1947. He had just officially accepted the ambulance on behalf of the St Agnes Division.

Members of the St John Ambulance, St Agnes Division, have their photograph taken with Mr T.E. Dunstan c. 1950. Back row (L to R): Douglas Mitchell, Cecil Tremain, Bill Woolcock and Mr Morse. Front row: Dr Henry Whitworth, Mr Dunstan and Alfie Kneebone.

In 1947 the Morris ambulance was replaced by a Vauxhall that had been converted from a private car by local garage owner Bill Dale. On Sunday the 11th May, the field owned by Dr W.C. Whitworth behind Vicarage Road was the scene of a special service conducted by the Rev. G.H. Barnicoat and the handing-over ceremony of the new ambulance. The vehicle was named 'St Agnes' by Miss Tremearne, whose family had contributed over half of the £925 needed to purchase the 26hp Vauxhall. Mr John King officially accepted the ambulance on behalf of the local Division.

Douglas Mitchell remembers the ambulance well: 'It had very light suspension, the crew and patients were often sick.' The vehicle was later sold to Christians the builders and Anthony Paull, who worked for Christians, said, 'It had seats along the side and the rear wheels were too far forward. When filled with workmen the front wheels almost lifted off the ground.' In the mid-1950s a four-man team consisting of Frank Roberts, Roy Lavin, Ray Johns and Alfie Kneebone competed in a competition in Redruth and won. Their instructor Dr Henry Whitworth was so pleased he bought the team a meal at the Cleaderscroft Hotel.

By 1954 Douglas Mitchell, Bill Woolcock and Cecil Tremain had joined the full-time ambulance service, taking away the experienced drivers. Douglas Mitchell believes that within 12 months the St Agnes Brigade folded. It is unclear what the building was then used for, but most people the writer has spoken to think it was possibly a store and in a bad state of repair. In 1973 the building was bought by the St Agnes Theatre Players for £1000. A *West Briton* newspaper article of the 5th April 1979 carried a report about the Players:

Last week saw the culmination of six years hard work, when their theatre workshop at Goonown was opened by Mr L. Carlyon, former headmaster of Blackwater School, who now lives in Launceston. It was created from the shell of a former ambulance hall, at a cost of more than £2,000. Grants came from Carrick District and St Agnes Parish Councils. The workshop provides a large heated rehearsal area, a storage area, a kitchen and toilet facilities. About 130 members, past members and guests, including Mr G. Williams, chairman of St Agnes Parish Council, and Mrs Williams were welcomed by Mr Tom Thewlis, president of the players. He introduced Mr L. Carlyon, the group's only life member. Mr Carlyon paid tribute to the late Mrs Daphne Dunstan, a former president, who died almost three years ago, and who for many years was the driving force behind the players' purchase of the hall.

The Theatre Players were formed in 1956 and were originally known as the Rosemundy House Players, staging their performances in the open air. In 1980 the workshop was the venue for their 25th birthday party, which was attended by past and present members.

The building today (2012) remains a store and rehearsal room for the Theatre Players.

The winning team at Redruth in the mid-1950s. Rear (L to R): Frank Roberts, Roy Lavin and Ray Johns. Alfie Kneebone holds the cup in the front.

St Agnes members of the St John Ambulance in the late 1950's, by which time Douglas Mitchell and Cecil Tremain had joined the full-time ambulance service and wear a different uniform. (L to R): Bert Skewes, Claude Lockett, Alfie Kneebone, Cecil Tremain, Roy Lavin and Douglas Mitchell shaking hands with Dr Henry Whitworth. Photo Ken Young.

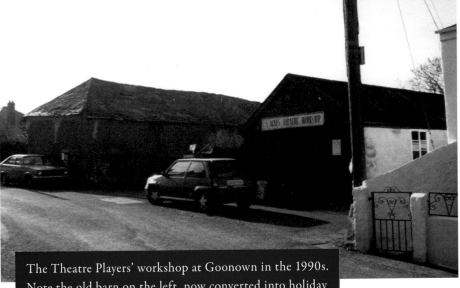

The Theatre Players' workshop at Goonown in the 1990s. Note the old barn on the left, now converted into holiday accommodation. It is believed that John Wesley preached from the steps of this barn on one of his many visits to St Agnes. This information has been passed down through many generations of the Butson family.

STE HARRIS, GOONOWN

Ste Harris with his butcher's wagon, seen earlier at Rosemundy, has now reached Goonown, where he stops again to allow local photographer Sammy Solway to take this picture around 1906. A man on the left saws a piece of wood on trestles outside Lawry's carpenter's shop. He is not going to stop his work while the picture is taken and therefore appears blurred.

On the right of the picture is a slightly taller building, the ground floor of which was for many years a shop run by Miss Dorothy Hooper. She appears in *Kelly's Trade Directory* as far back as 1910. Frank Roberts remembered the shop: 'Dot Hooper had the lock-up shop and she sold groceries in one room downstairs. The upstairs I believe was part of the cottage next door. It had a little shop window at the front.' Barbara Kent (née Geach) also remembered

the shop: 'Dot Hooper sold sweets, candles, soap powder and Puritan soap and everything smelt of paraffin.'

Colin Butson remembers that on the end of the building there were two large metal advertising boards, at which they threw stones as children. Colin's sister Margaret believes the shop was there until it closed in the early 1950s, but Dot returned daily to feed her cats. At the other end of this row of cottages (to the rear of the butcher's wagon) there was for many years a small building used as a cobbler's shop by John Henry Cayzer. On the 1881 census he is shown living at Goonown with his occupation a cordwainer (shoemaker). In the 1891 census his occupation is a boot maker. Among Maurice Bizley's notes (though not used in his book *Friendly Retreat*) is the following passage: 'The cobblers shop must have been very similar to 'Penticosts' in Charles Lee's book *Our Little Town* and Mr Cayzer appears to have been a character fit for any book.' Frank Roberts and his sister Irene were related to John Henry Cayzer, and Irene, now aged 107, recalled him there. She called him Uncle John. The entrance to his shop looked down the road towards Rosemundy and she remembered seeing her father in the building when she came home from school. Her father, John Henry Roberts, learnt the cobbling trade with him and later he started his own cobbler's business in a shed in the garden of number 32 where he lived and where Frank lives today. The date he started is unclear but it was before Frank was born so it was probably around the First World War when John Henry Cayzer was retirement age. It seems likely that John Roberts took over his business.

During the Second World War John Cayzer's old building was used by Bill Woolcock as a cobbler's shop. His daughter Irene Scoble said, 'He had it for several years. During the war he had the contract to repair soldiers' boots stationed at Cameron Camp.'

GOONOWN CHAPEL

The Methodist movement began in the eighteenth century, and John Wesley and his associates very soon began to visit Cornwall. Between 1743 and 1787 he travelled to Cornwall thirty-two times, exhausting journeys of about six days on horseback, requiring frequent stops. Small meetings were held in people's houses, while large groups met in the open air. Gradually, chapels were built and the Wesleyan Methodists were formed.

John Wesley made nineteen visits to St Agnes during this period, and on his seventh visit in 1760 he wrote in his journal: 'The congregation at St Agnes in the evening was, I suppose, double that at Port Isaac. We had near as many on Tuesday the 9th at five in the morning, as the Preaching House could contain.' Later, during his seventeenth visit, he wrote on the 18th August 1776: 'The passage through the sands (journey from Cubert) being bad for a chaise, I rode on horseback to St Agnes, where the rain constrained me to preach in the house.' These entries suggest that as early as 1760 there was a building somewhere in St Agnes used as a meeting house, or 'preaching house' as Wesley preferred to call it. Its location unfortunately is not known.

In his *Chronological History of the People called Methodists*, W. Myles gives 1780 as the date of the first Methodist chapel in St Agnes. On the flyleaf of the *Goonown Chapel Trust Account Book* of 1838, however, is written: 'Goonown Chapel erected 1790'. This date is then crossed out and 'or 1785' added in different handwriting and ink.

The correct date is important. Tradition has it that John Wesley, aged 82 years, preached in this chapel on his nineteenth and last visit to St Agnes in 1785. He wrote in his journal: 'At half-past eight I preached at St Agnes to the largest congregation I ever saw there', but it is quite clear that if the chapel was built in 1790 he could not have preached in this building. Was the date 1790 altered on the account book cover to make the dates fit? Or was it because it was known at the time that John Wesley did preach here and therefore the original date of 1790 was wrong? We may never know, but it is quite possible that the great preacher did speak at Goonown Chapel. We do know that the chapel cost £500 to build and there were seventeen trustees.

In 1809 a Methodist Sunday School was formed, which was to remain here for 130 years.

The record books of the Goonown Chapel Trust, held at the County Record Office in Truro, give an interesting picture of the early years of this chapel. The earliest minute book, commencing in October 1838, names the Chapel Trustees: Stephen Dale, James Angwin, James Evans, James Prout, Samuel Pearce, Joseph Ninnis, Francis Rowe, Stephen Martin, Thomas Martin, James Stephens, Edward Woolcock, Richard Rowe, William Rowe, Thomas Gill, Thomas M. Ninnis, Thomas Rowse, John Nancarrow.

In the *Journal of John Carter (1835-1907)*, the author wrote:

I was taken to the Goonown Sunday School when about five years old [c. 1840]. The leading men there in my early days were George Rogers, Thomas Whitta, Capt. Joseph Ninnis, Thomas Ninnis, James Stephens and others. In that school many characters were made, scores of young men were moulded and fashioned to a large extent for responsible positions in various parts of the world and so they have gone out to almost every part of the habitable globe doing credit to their homes and all their early surroundings. ... We had no organ there but generally there would be one or more flutes, sometimes a clarinet, one or two bass-viols, a trombone and serpent but I never knew a violin in church worship in Cornwall. ... All this time I was a very regular attendant at the Goonown Sunday School and for a good while was in the Bible Class, my near associates were William Endean of Truro, William Webb and John Hosking of Polbreen, Captain Joseph Ninnis and Thomas Ninnis were my teachers. George Rogers was the Superintendent, our school numbered over three hundred scholars and about fifty teachers.

One of the largest items of expenditure was the purchase of tallow candles for lighting. In 1838 they were 9/- (45p) a dozen, decreasing to 6/- (30p) in 1845. Then from 1846 the price slowly increased again until it reached 10/- (50p) in 1855, and from then until 1860 it was about 9/-. Snuffers for the candles, made by the local blacksmith, cost 1/7d. (about 8p) for three pairs. Water was purchased at 2/- (10p) a year from a neighbouring well owner.

On the 1st November 1851 the chapel was registered for the solemnizing of marriages, and on Christmas Day 1852, Sol Paull James was presented with a Bible and hymn book on his marriage, it being the first solemnized in the chapel. In June 1852 it was resolved that a new vestry be erected forthwith for accommodating the classes. In May 1858 the Trust bought land in the centre of St Agnes from the Bryannack Estate, and it was on this land that the new Wesleyan chapel was to be built.

Nineteen trustees were appointed for the new chapel and at their first meeting, held on the 18th April 1860, it was resolved that the building would be proceeded with. The new chapel was completed and opened for divine service on Wednesday the 18th June 1862.

1859 Sunday School Jubilee medal.

In 1859 the Sunday School had celebrated its jubilee, and special jubilee medals were made to celebrate the event.

In 1862 Goonown Chapel, with its congregation now worshipping at their new building in British Road, became the permanent home of the St Agnes Methodist Sunday School, better known as Goonown Sunday School.

At a Trust meeting in August 1867 the chairman stated that Messrs Oates of Blackwater had made application for the use of the Goonown vestry for a day school, and it was resolved that they be allowed to use it on weekdays (some evenings excepted) until 1869. They had to pay 2/6d (12½p) per quarter towards upkeep.

In October 1870 the first public meeting was held at Goonown following the re-establishment of the Band of Hope. The Band of Hope was founded in 1847 by Jabez Tunnicliff for all children under 16 years, based on a simple pledge: 'I do agree that I will not use intoxicating liquor as beverages.' Some societies even mentioned tobacco, snuff and opium. Many of them started within existing Sunday Schools. At the meeting at Goonown, presided over by Mr W. Butson, addresses were delivered to a large audience by E. Vivian, W.J. Kernick, T. Curnow and W. Letcher. About 14 signed the pledge.

By 1873 only Thomas Rowse, John Nancarrow and Thomas Ninnis remained of the old trustees, and the following new trustees were appointed: James Rogers – Draper and Grocer; James Letcher – Miner; Henry Peters – Miner; Joel Hooper – Miner; Richard Stribley – Farmer; John Williams – Mine Agent; Nics. Langdon – Builder; Wm. Butson – Yeoman; Rd. Rickard – Miner; Thos. Stribley – Shopkeeper; Geo. Tregellas – Blacksmith; Thos. Stephens – Engineer; Walter Letcher – Silversmith; Robt. M. James – Farmer; Jos. Tremewan – Shopkeeper; Thos. Carter – Miner; James Rogers, Jnr. – Grocer.

The Sunday School continued into the 20th century but by now the building was over 100 years old and in need of repair. The *Royal Cornwall Gazette* of the 14th January 1904 reported: 'Sir Edwin Durning Lawrence has given a donation of two guineas towards renovation of Goonown Sunday School.'

Tea Treats were held annually by both the Sunday School and the Band of Hope, who sometimes called theirs a demonstration. It seems that although the two events were organised by separate groups, many children attended both. They were big occasions, at which the children and teachers, some carrying banners and flags, paraded around the village led by a local brass band and ending up in a friendly farmer's field or other suitable area of land. Games were played and large quantities of tea and saffron cake consumed. The Sunday School Tea Treat usually took place in a field in Penwinnick Road, where Penwinnick Parc is today, but for a few years towards the end of the First World War and just after it, the event was held in the small field opposite Coulterville (Cleaderscroft) in British Road, kindly loaned by Mr Coulter Hancock. The Band of Hope also paraded around the village, but they ended

The Band of Hope Tea Treat in
Mr Arthur Butson's field in 1907.

up in a field adjoining Goonown Farm, owned by the Butson family.
Like today, fine weather could not be guaranteed, and on Saturday the 19th
July 1902 the Tea Treat was postponed because of stormy and wet weather.
It was held on the following Monday afternoon, and the schoolchildren were
given the afternoon off to attend.

In May 1907 the *Royal Cornwall Gazette* reported: 'The annual
demonstration of the Goonown Band of Hope took place on Whit Monday.
Headed by Trevince Band, the members paraded the streets and afterwards
partook of tea in the open. The evening meeting was presided over by
councillor Fellowes of Wolverhampton and addresses were given by the Revs
G.W. Thompson, W.G. Corke and Mr M.J. Angwin.'

The year 1909 was a big one for the Sunday School as it celebrated its
100th anniversary. Again a medal was made to celebrate the occasion, and
that summer's annual tea was a particularly special event. The *Royal Cornwall
Gazette* of the 22nd July reported: 'On Saturday, large numbers of old scholars
joined the procession as it was part of the centenary celebrations, the school
having been started in 1809. Scholars under eighteen were given a free tea and

officers, teachers and scholars were each presented with a
medal which was specially struck for the occasion. Truro
territorial band and St Agnes town band rendered a choice
selection of instrumental music during the afternoon and
evening.'

In July 1910 the weather was again unkind, the
Royal Cornwall Gazette reporting: 'Wet weather on
Saturday sadly interfered with the success of the Wesleyan
Sunday School tea. Two bands were engaged, St Agnes
Town and St Dennis.' The following year, Illogan Band
under the Rev. Mr Oxland was one of the attractions,
which also included singing and reciting competitions,
maypole dances and sports. Illogan Band under the same
bandmaster attended again in 1912, the event being held
in a field at Penwinnick loaned by Mr Peters.

Centenary medal.

The July 1913 Sunday School Tea Treat procession
was a 'garland' occasion and the *Royal Cornwall Gazette* reported that 'various
shapes and sizes of garlands of beautiful flowers made a very pretty sight. Tea
was provided in a field at Penwinnick, kindly loaned by Mr Peters, the children
having their tea free through the generosity of former scholars at home and in
South Africa. Sports were arranged for the young people and St Dennis band
contributed a capital programme.'

In June 1914 the Band of Hope Festival was held and the *West Briton*
carried this report: 'St Agnes Band of Hope Festival was held on Whit Monday
under favourable circumstances. The children met in Goonown schoolroom
and after a hymn and prayer the children formed a procession headed by
St Agnes Band and paraded the principal streets. Through the kindness of
Mr and Mrs Adkin they were permitted to enter the beautiful grounds of
Rosemundy. On returning to a field at Goonown lent by Mr A. Butson the
children were provided with buns and at 5 o'clock a public tea was provided.'
A month later, in July, the Sunday School held their own Tea Treat, but it was
not as successful as the Band of Hope's. The *Royal Cornwall Gazette* reported

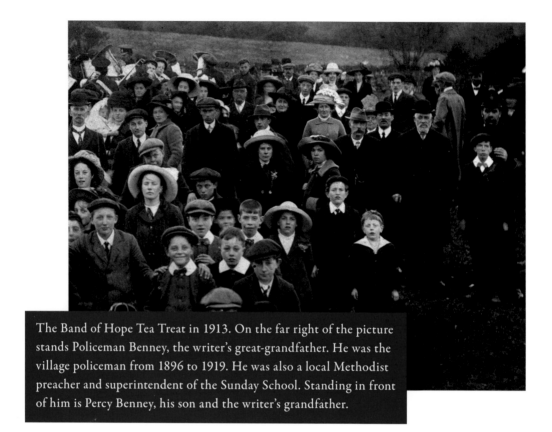

The Band of Hope Tea Treat in 1913. On the far right of the picture stands Policeman Benney, the writer's great-grandfather. He was the village policeman from 1896 to 1919. He was also a local Methodist preacher and superintendent of the Sunday School. Standing in front of him is Percy Benney, his son and the writer's grandfather.

that it was partially spoilt by rain in the early afternoon. Furthermore, 'The procession was below average and the counter attractions drew the children away from the field and games.' It does not say what the 'counter attractions' were.

On the 20th August 1919 the *Royal Cornwall Gazette* reported: 'The annual gathering on Friday of the Methodist Sunday School was a great success. There was the usual procession, headed by St Agnes Band under Mr H. Robins around the grounds of Rosemundy and the principal streets to the field lent by Mr G.C. Hancock where tea was served. A free tea was provided for the children and the ex-servicemen, whilst the older members of the church and the sick were not forgotten. In the sports that followed the young people thoroughly enjoyed themselves.'

c. 1913: a group of adults and children at the Band of Hope Tea Treat in Arthur Butson's field at Goonown. The man in the middle, with the white beard, is George Gerry, a fisherman, who attended the Tea Treats selling what he called 'Rock Beef', which was actually limpets. Many people in the photo are eating limpets out of shells, including Policeman Benney. He stands on the left with a shell in his left hand and a limpet in his right. To the left of Policeman Benney, in the large hat, is Beatty Delbridge, and to her left, eating limpets, is Capt. Dick Waters. On his left is John Lawry, who stands beside Harry Stribley, both also eating limpets. Behind Harry Stribley is John May and to his left, slightly side on, is Charlie Uren. The row continues with John Osborne, Charlie James, John Berryman and John Tredinnick, with the white beard. In the front row, kneeling or sitting, are Edith Lawry on George Gerry's right and Thomas John Delbridge and Jim Lawry to his left. The large house in the background is number 17 Goonown, at the end of Goonown Lane.

The Band of Hope tea in 1915. Everyone is wearing a hat except one boy in the front row who has taken off his cap for the photo.

St. Agnes Wes. Band of Hope Tea 1915

The Sunday School Tea Treats continued to be held in the field off Penwinnick Road until the 1950s when outings were introduced, which usually meant a trip to Carbis Bay. By this time of course the Sunday School itself had moved from Goonown to the chapel in British Road, but in the first half of the 20th century Goonown Chapel remained the centre of many Methodist activities in the village's religious and social life, including Harvest Suppers, Tea Treats, concerts, pantomimes, bazaars and jumble sales. The chapel building, standing at the western end of Goonown Lane, was 75 ft. long by 66 ft. wide, with a double-ridged roof. There was a gallery, and the main hall had a seating capacity of approximately 300 people, making it the largest hall in St Agnes.

During the Second World War of 1939-1945 St Agnes played host to many evacuees. Halls and large rooms suitable for classrooms were in great demand. Goonown was one of those considered but was rejected on the grounds that the toilet facilities were unsuitable. (They consisted of one WC and an outside urinal.)

The old Goonown Chapel had ceased to be a home to the Sunday School from the outbreak of the Second World War, and in October 1940 local builder Albert Reynolds charged £2 18s 4d (about £2.91½p) to clear the building. This included 10/- (50p) to hire a lorry and £2 8s 4d (about £2.41½p) for labour and labourers. In 1943 when there was a considerable build-up of troops in Cornwall prior to the D-Day landings, Goonown Chapel, which was standing empty, was commandeered as a billet for American forces. Margaret Davey remembers the hall being used by soldiers returning after Dunkirk and described many of the men as being in 'rags and tatters'. The inside of the building was left in a poor condition.

In 1949 Phil Taylor was the big mover in the formation of a badminton club. Albert Reynolds and Ronnie Jeffery carried out repairs to the hall and it was painted by club members. The club became very successful and the team members were awarded the South West Shield 1953/54 as the unbeaten league winners.

The badminton club 1953/54. Rear (L to R): Ron Rogers, Nancy Kellow, Brenchley Cornish, Rex Truan, Phil Taylor, Tony Birch, Horton Davey, Frank Dunstan, Della Rogers and Freddie Nicholls. Front: Daphne Dunstan, Beatrice (Beatty) Cornish, Ada Oats, Ruby Nicholls, Margaret Davey, Emmie ? and Elsie Vanstone.

St Agnes Methodist Church Christmas fair on the 26th November 1955. The fair was opened by Mrs A. Walters of Mount Hawke and the money raised was for a new piano. This photograph shows the butterfly competition, with Hilary Renfree, Carol Jeffery (rear of head), Phyllis Butson, Muriel Kneebone, Ewart Butson, unknown and Colin Butson.

The building continued to be used by the community for social events, and well attended concerts were also held in the hall. Colin Butson said, 'This was the largest public hall in St Agnes; it had a balcony and big concerts were held there. The stage was stored in a room adjoining the hall and constructed for each event. The gallery was eventually condemned.'

The Boys' Brigade at their first anniversary celebration, around 1960. Men standing (L to R): Rev. Joe Ridholls, Mr John Winter (helper), Mr Rex Trewartha (helper) and Ian Frank (County Youth Officer). Far side of table: Roger Hughes, Barry Spring, Robert Glover, Michael Glover, Peter Glover, unknown, Malcolm Carveth, Tony Williams, Kingsley Thomas, unknown, Neil Roberts and Bryn Chaplin. Nearside of table: unknown, Ewart Butson, Anthony Thomas, Paddy Spring, ? Luke, Nigel Trewartha, Robert Sowden, David Prime and Malcolm Windsor. Photo Ken Young.

Around 1959 the St Agnes Methodist minister, Joe Ridholls, with the help of Daphne Dunstan, formed a youth club at the hall. As many as 60 youngsters attended each week. The children were split into four groups, each doing different activities, including football, table tennis, gymnastics and handicraft. The groups would alternate activities during the evening. Joe also started a Boys' Brigade company. It was Church-based, and during their meetings they had drill, did various activities and finished the evening with a prayer. Joe left St Agnes in 1962, and the local youth club and Boys' Brigade ended shortly afterwards. The St Agnes Cubs also used the hall for meetings.

In 1963 the building was sold to Mr Norman Coad who converted it into three flats, each with a garage.

Goonown Chapel in 2007, converted into flats.

ST AGNES FEAST DAY

Feast Monday, the nearest Monday to January 21st, was a highlight of the year with the Church and Chapel having their own special celebrations. The Church had theirs in the Church Hall with songs, monologues etc., then it finished with a dance. Margaret Davey in *The St Agnes Museum Journal No. 16,* wrote that the Chapel events were 'more sedate' than the Church and consisted of a 'Feast Tea, a sumptuous spread (Wesleyans were noted for their teas and suppers). A concert in Goonown School-room, a large building with a hallway ... The heating was an ancient Tortoise stove, we went well wrapped up; we were a hardy race in those days!'

In January 1955 the Feast Dinner had a Victorian theme and many people dressed up to join in the celebration. Local photographer Ken Young attended and recorded the event in a series of photographs.

Feast Dinner 1955. Nearside of table: Anne Chappell, Marlene Skewes, Ron Jeffery, Hilda Roberts, Frank Dunstan, Mrs Fleming, unknown, Muriel Kneebone, Rev. Ambrose Payne, Florrie Trezise, John Thomas and Margaret Davey. Far side of table: unknown, Albert Reynolds, Mrs Butcher, Brenchley Cornish, Margaret Roberts (née Pope), Daphne Dunstan, Luther Stephens, Edith Shrimpton (née Pope), Clyde Pope, Kathleen Boundy, David James, Freda Reynolds, Mr Butcher, Margaret Thomas and Mrs Tom Dunstan. Among the people behind the table on the left are Ethel Borlase, Ada Oats and Mrs Sandercock.

Feast Dinner 1955. Head of the table is Mrs Tom Dunstan. Left of table (front to rear): Elizabeth Pugsley (née Thomas), Doris Ward (née Angwin), Frank Kneebone, Margaret Davey, Lester Roberts, unknown, John Thomas, Florrie Trezise, Rev. Ambrose Payne, Muriel Kneebone. Right of table (front to rear): Margaret Thomas, Mr Butcher, Freda Reynolds, David James, Kathleen Boundy, Clyde Pope, Edith Shrimpton, Luther Stephens, Daphne Dunstan, Margaret Roberts, Brenchley Cornish, Mrs Butcher, Albert Reynolds, unknown.

Feast Dinner 1955. Left of table: Jeanette Trezise, Margaret Payne, Elsie Vanstone, Kay Thewlis, Beatty Cornish, Horton Davey and Margaret Butson. At the end of the table is Chris Williams with Donald Tremain behind him. Right of table (front to rear): unknown, Mrs Ennor, James Thomas, David Boundy, Maralyn Weeway, Geoffrey Roberts, Terri Greenbank, Roger Williams, Susan Pope and Elizabeth Williams. On the tables to the right are Ursula Lampshire, Austin Trezise, Frank Williams, Marjorie Williams, Daphne Blight, May Richards and Maureen Blight. Far side of table are Stanley Williams, Mrs Tallack, Florence Pope, Rex Truan, Miss Wood, Mrs Miller and Marion Stribley.

Feast Dinner 1955. Standing (L to R): Luther Stephens, Daphne Dunstan, Hilda Roberts, Ron Jeffery, Mrs Butcher, Albert Reynolds and Freda Reynolds. Seated: Ambrose Payne.

Feast Dinner 1955. (L to R): Lester Roberts, Margaret Davey, Margaret Roberts, Brenchley Cornish, Beatrice (Beatty) Cornish and Horton Davey.

GOONOWN FOOTBALL CLUB

The Goonown club is first mentioned in the *West Briton* on the 12th September 1901: 'The newly-formed Goonown Football Club opened the season with a practice game last Saturday, in which some good form was shown.' In November 1901 the *Cornish Post and Mining News* reported on a game between Goonown and Africanders. The teams consisted of:

Africanders

Hodge

Gribben   C. Harper

Rilstone   Dunstan (Capt.)   Weston

W. Williams   Tredinnick   Billing   Roberts   Tregellas

Goonown

Halls

Delbridge   G.S. Roberts

Varker   Prout (Capt.)   Rowe

Wills   Bennetts   Cock   Mitchell   Hooper

Goonown lost 5-3 and the paper reported:

> An exciting encounter in which Captain Dunstan, late of West Coast,
> shined as brilliantly as the midday sun. There is one thing which strikes
> me as being somewhat extraordinary. I wonder why Captain Dunstan
> named his men 'Africanders'. True he and Hodge have been to south and
> other parts of Africa but just look at the others! How long have 'Billing
> and Co' returned from Wild West? But what's in a name? They won, and
> all South African boys will learn with pleasure that Captain Dunstan
> has been such a successful instructor in the difficult art of goal kicking.

On the 5th December the *Cornish Post and Mining News* reported on
Goonown's match with Perranporth: 'Played at Goonown on Saturday, it was
witnessed by a large number. The visitors proved themselves the better side
and retired winners by 3 goals to 1.' In October 1902 Goonown beat
St Agnes reserves 6-0 but on the 23rd of that month the *West Briton*
reported: 'Goonown travelled to Probus on Saturday but the village team
easily accounted for them to the tune of 5 goals to nil.' The following week
they lost 4-3 at home to St John's, Truro, and on the 13th November 1902 the
West Briton reported: 'St Georges visited Goonown on Friday and suffered
a defeat of 3 goals to nil.' On the 24th January 1903 Goonown played Truro
St John's again but no result is shown. On the 12th February the *Cornubian
and Redruth Times* reported that Goonown beat Goonown reserves 6-0.
In October 1903 Goonown lent their pitch and a ball to the Goonvrea team
to play Wheal Busy but after a few minutes' play the ball burst and the game
had to be stopped. No further mention of the club has been found in any
newspaper after this date.

GOONOWN
PLAYING FIELD

The *Royal Cornwall Gazette* of the 29th August 1928 included a long article announcing the opening ceremony of the playing field, under the heading 'Sports Ground for St Agnes', and with a subheading 'Protecting youngsters from the dangers of the road' the paper stated:

The triumphant conclusion of a scheme to provide a playing field for St Agnes was signalled on Saturday, when a well laid-out and equipped recreation ground was opened by Dr Allan Hancock. St Agnes shares with most Cornish villages the incessant menace of high speed motor traffic to the safety of the children, and the idea of providing a recreation ground was enthusiastically taken up by a local branch of the National Playing Fields Association, and pushed forward as expeditiously as possible. The Association were hindered by several failures to get the land, but eventually the difficulty was met by buying, for £200, a two acre field at Goonown. In connection with the opening ceremony on Saturday an attractive programme was arranged, including sports, boxing matches and an open air dance. ... Declaring the ground open, Dr. Allan Hancock said he had heard criticism of the selection of the field at Goonown. He dissented from that criticism, because while the children of that district – and there were a good many of them – had no place but the road to play in, the children of the town area could play on the beach. He was glad that in the laying out of the new ground the first thought had been for the children, and cricket and football had been put somewhat in the background. He also favoured the provision of a sand pit which would be appreciated by the mothers who would also be able to get some fresh air whilst looking after their children.

Sports were then held, followed by a public tea.

St Agnes football team and committee 1929/30, winners of the St Columb and
District League. They played their home games at Goonown playing field.
Back row (L to R): George Higgins, Henry Jennings, Micky Langford, Bill
Sandercock, Arthur Spring, Dick Whitford, Solomon.
Middle row (L to R): Johnny Carveth, Bill Harris, Ralph Butson, Rex Richards,
A. Tonkin, Freddie Harper, Johnny Mitchell.
Front row (L to R): Lish Whitford, Wilfred Carveth, Cecil Borlase, Bert Spring,
Acland Bennetts.

In December 1928 local builder Albert Reynolds erected goalposts on
the field at a cost of £2 12s 6d (£2.62½p). The following year, for the 1929/30
season, and for the next three years, St Agnes Football Club played their home
matches here. Records show that they paid £4 a year in rent to use the pitch.
This however was not an ideal location as the ball damaged the roofs of houses
alongside the ground. To stay there the club had to erect a high netting fence
and they could not afford this expense. By the 1933/34 season they had moved
to a new ground at Ropewalk, Goonbell.

In July 1930 Albert Reynolds was given the job of painting the swings, entrance gates and goalposts for a second opening of the field. It is almost certain that this event two years later was to inaugurate the new play equipment and the new shelter and pavilion erected during the intervening two years, since the *West Briton* of the 17th October 1929 had reported that the committee of the St Agnes Playing Field Association had accepted Charles Harper's tender of £76 for erecting the pavilion. (At this time part of the field was enclosed for the use of the football team.) The second opening was also well reported in the *Royal Cornwall Gazette* (30th July 1930):

> The new playing field which has been provided for the Parish was opened on Saturday by Lady Carkeek. It is largely through the kindness of Major Gilpin, who advanced the purchase money £204 free of interest, that the ground has been secured. It is two and a quarter acres in extent. The shelter and pavilion has been provided by Mr. W.J. Mills of Torquay; the Angwin family has given the entrance gates, and Maj. and Mrs Gilpin have erected swings, etc. for the children. At the opening ceremony, Maj. Gilpin presiding, dedicatory prayers were said by the vicar Rev. W.H. Browne. Lady Carkeek formally declared the field open and little Daphne Roberts presented her ladyship with a bouquet.

From its opening to the present day the playing field and apparatus have been well used, and over the years the ground has been home to many activities, including circuses, fairs, football, pushball, hockey and school sports days, to name just a few.

Austin Tremain remembers it being used by American servicemen during the war to play baseball. They marched from their camp at Penwinnick Road to the playing field, chanting songs as they went. Austin said, 'One very large black American said to me, "I eat little boys like you" – I ran.'

In the mid-1950s Colin Butson remembers Hazzards Circus coming to the playing field: he described it as a 'lash-up' circus. The Goonown Sunday School Tea Treat had been cancelled because of rain and the children were taken to the circus instead. The tent leaked badly and people had umbrellas up inside the tent. The only animals Colin could remember were a donkey, horse

Major Gilpin presiding over the opening of Goonown playing field in 1930.

The new pavilion c. 1930. The left-hand side was a small room for the caretaker. The centre and right side were seated areas, the seats in the latter area facing towards the gate.

The pushball match at Goonown. Each team tries to lift the ball off the ground and take it to the opponents' goal.

The teams stand or sit beside the *Daily Mail* pushball at Goonown c. 1930.

The ladies' hockey team at Goonown c. 1946. Rear (L to R): Nancy James, Margaret Till, Phyllis Robinson, Elizabeth Dunne, Ada Oats, Elsie Vanstone and Steph Wilson. Front: ? Jones, Nita Twiss, Betty Heyworth and Margaret Davey.

and monkey. Fairs were also common in the 1950s, consisting of sideshows, dodgems, swing boats and other children's rides.

After the War and until St Agnes School had its own sports field at the new school, sports days were held here. In 1965 athlete Diane Charles (née Leathers), presented the cups and prizes to the winners. She was the first lady to run the mile under 5 minutes. She brought with her the three medals that fellow athlete Mary Rand had won in the 1964 Olympic Games in Tokyo: gold for the long jump, silver for the pentathlon and bronze for the 4x100 relay. Mary Rand was the first-ever British female athlete to win an Olympic gold medal in track and field and her long jump of 6.76 metres was a world record. The following year, 1966, Mary Rand came herself and presented the cups and prizes. She even competed in the mothers' race and despite giving the mothers a head start she still managed to win.

Today the field continues to be well used and is maintained and cared for by a keen management committee.

Sports day winners and teachers c. 1949. (L to R): Yvonne Brown, Mr Baker, Mr Hearn, unknown, Mr Andain, Mr Jones and David Drew.

Sports day winners in 1965 with Mary Rand's Olympic medals on the table. Back row (L to R): Sue Hockings, Clive Benney, Rhoderick Mitchell, Diane Charles, Richard Bamber, Sarah James and Mandy Foot. Photo Ken Young.

Sports day winners in 1966 with Olympic champion Mary Rand. (L to R): Hilary Moyle, Robin Williams, Debbie Mitchell, Mary Rand, Dean Woon, Brian Roberts, Sarah James and Andrew Beckett. Photo Ken Young.

Olympic long jump champion Mary Rand, far left, competes in the mothers' race at the 1966 school sports day. Photo Ken Young.

GOONOWN & THE GREENY

GOONOWN ST.AGNES.   No.3

Cottages at Goonown c. 1913, before the addition of extensions and porches. In the late 1980s Mr Hugo Smith and his sister sent an audio tape and letter to the writer with information about St Agnes and this photograph. Hugo Smith is sitting on the road with a milk can between his legs and his sister stands on his right with her hands clasped.

Adults and children stand in line across the road at Goonown around 1913.

The following information also came from Hugo Smith and his sister:

In the right background are Police Constable May and wife in the garden. In the centre is Mr Wales. Edna Pearce is holding her nephew. The tall girl is Millie Lobb and Phyllis May is holding the hand of Florence Dawson. In the middle, the older girl's surname is Hotwell; she is with Madeline Gribben. On the left near shop [brick building abutting the road] is Miss James. My brother Joseph Smith holds the broom and old Mr Andrew is with the dog. Mr Andrew had the farm on the right. The white building without a chimney was part of his farm where the cowsheds were. He lived on the other side of the road. We called him 'Smock-up' Andrew. My brother Joseph went everywhere with 'Smock-up' – he took him under his wing.

Frank Roberts remembered the area a little later:

> Tom Bennetts lived in the white cottage on the right. He had a horse and
> cart with a tank on the back and sold paraffin. He had a shed in the field
> below the playing field that he used for his horse and as a store.

The large building on the left was Joseph Roberts' house. The little brick
building on the end was built by him for his daughter Edith James as a shop
when her husband, a miner, was killed. Frank Roberts said, 'It was just a shop
run by Aunt Edith for a few years as far as I know. No-one took it over and it
just closed.'

This view taken about 1906 shows, in the foreground, a
narrow, grassy piece of land known as the Greeny.
Several bungalows now stand here but at this time it was
a natural playing field for the children of the village.

A dog show at Goonown around 1940. Austin Trezise stands on the left with his St Bernard. Austin was a founder member of the St Agnes dog show. As well as St Bernards he also showed Great Danes and boxers.

In the book *Friendly Retreat* Maurice Bizley writes: 'In the wall opposite the Greeny grows that succulent plant with flat, circular leaves, the Cornish pennywort (cotyledon umbilicus), well known by the name of "Penny Pies." There is an interesting old remedy for chilblains in this district, concocted by mixing lard with the leaves of Penny Pies after they have been pounded to a pulp.' Unfortunately, with the building of the new bungalows on that side of the road, residents must now go elsewhere for their cure.

GOONBELL

It is not that easy to decide where Goonown ends and Goonbell begins, but by the telephone kiosk at Head Lane seems the most likely spot. The name Goonbell comprises the Cornish words 'goon' (= 'down') and 'pell' (= 'far off, distant'): Distant Down. This would seem to be an appropriate name, since early maps show some houses at Goonown and Head Lane but from here as far as Chiverton the land was totally unenclosed, open commons or downs.

Head Lane, the small dead-end lane beside the telephone kiosk at Goonbell, was, before the arrival of the railway line through Goonbell, the thoroughfare which connected the area to Penwinnick Road. With the coming of the railway, however, the road was diverted alongside the new track and came out further up the road opposite the Wheal Butson junction. The area around Head Lane is known to older local people as 'Hill 60'. The original Hill 60, near Ypres in Flanders, was the scene of fierce fighting in the Great War, and the name was given to this part of St Agnes because it was once notorious for being a rough area, as Frank Roberts confirms. A panel inside the telephone kiosk still (2012) shows Hill 60 as its location.

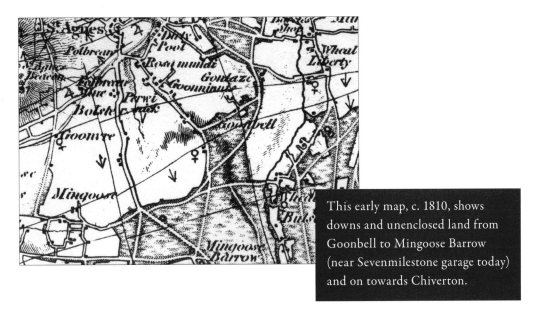

This early map, c. 1810, shows downs and unenclosed land from Goonbell to Mingoose Barrow (near Sevenmilestone garage today) and on towards Chiverton.

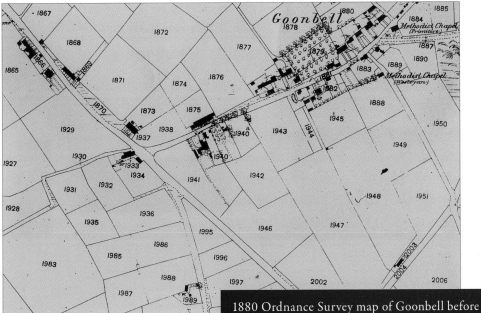

1880 Ordnance Survey map of Goonbell before the arrival of the railway. The road to Penwinnick is via Head Lane, where the telephone kiosk stands today. Note also the two Methodist chapels in the top right of the map and the area known as the 'Greeny', numbered 1870.

GOONBELL POST OFFICE AND SHOP

As far back as 1935 Goonbell had its own post office. The *Royal Cornwall Gazette* of the 5th September 1935 reported: 'A post office was opened at Goonbell on Monday. This district is becoming extremely popular'. Originally the post office was in a flat-roofed building attached to the bungalow to the left of the grocer's shop. The first sub-postmistress was Mrs Cole, who was replaced in 1940 by Mr Heath. He remained here until 1946.

In 1946 the post office moved into the grocer's shop next door, and the bungalow and old post office building were occupied by Mr and Mrs Ron Luke. Mrs Luke told the writer that the shop next door to her became the post office and was owned by Arthur Thomas, but she described it as 'downtrodden'. She said that in the evenings her husband Ron would spend one or two hours in the old post office part of their new home heeling boots and shoes. He had been trained by his uncle Alf James.

Arthur Thomas' shop next door, which became the post office, had been a shop as far back as 1910 and probably long before. Trade directories of 1893 have Joseph Prout as a grocer in Goonbell, and it seems likely that these were his premises. From 1910 to 1930 Mrs Bessie Gribben was the shopkeeper here, followed in the early 1930s by Miss Laurel Gribben and (by 1939) Arthur Thomas. In 1946 when the post office moved from the bungalow into this shop, Miss Kate Thomas was the sub-postmistress. It remained a post office and stores under several different sub-postmasters until its closure in the late 1990s.

Today, 2012, a two-storey house stands on the site.

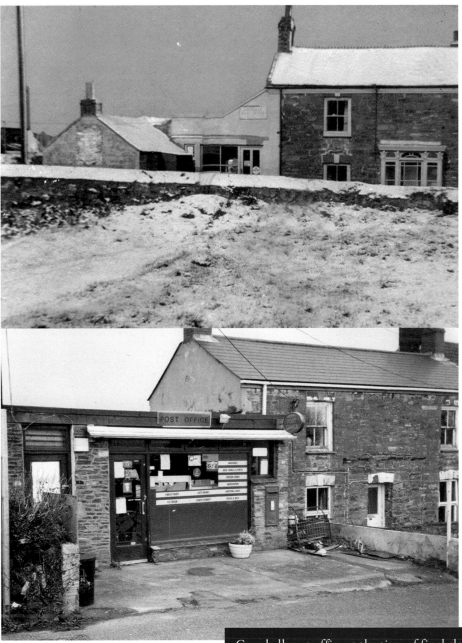

Goonbell post office in January 1967. Photo Alan Green.

Goonbell post office at the time of final closure.

c. 1910: a small girl stands in the road, holding a pitcher in her right hand and a watering can in her left. She has probably just collected or is going to collect water from one of the standpipes in the Goonbell area.

Delbridge's baker's wagon outside Avonlea c. 1908. Thomas John Delbridge was the baker in St Agnes at this time and the young delivery boy poses beside the wagon. The writing on the side describes Mr Delbridge as a 'Scientific Baker'.

An unusual view of Goonbell around 1906.

The large house on the right (above) called Avonlea, was occupied by Edward Trezise and his wife Evelyn.

Edward, a butcher, started his business in 1895 at Promised Land (originally called Promise Land) and using a pony-drawn vehicle, travelled the area selling meat which he bought at Redruth. His trade grew, and he moved to Avonlea to carry on his growing business, using his own slaughterhouse. In 1903 Edward and Evelyn had a son, Austin. As Austin grew up he would help his father in his business and even deliver meat before going to school.

The thatched cottages on the left of the picture were demolished in the early 1900s, and in 1923 Edward and Austin built a new house on the site and named it Tresleigh. After leaving school Austin went to work for his father, slaughtering and delivering their own meat. The slaughtering stopped during the 1939-1945 War when rationed supplies could only be bought from an authorised central depot. On the death of his father in 1944 Austin continued to run the business on his own, buying meat from the abattoir. He never had a shop but people would come to the yard to buy meat from him. He retired in 1969.

Edward Trezise on the left and Austin on the far right, in the 1930s, lean against a converted car or lorry that was used as a tractor on the farm. To help with grip, blocks of concrete have been placed on the rear and rope wrapped around the tyres. Many local farmers had vehicles like this to assist them on their farms.

Austin Trezise with his butcher's wagon, c. 1940.

Photographer H.D. Wootton from Redruth took this view of Goonbell c. 1908.

A view down through Goonbell in the 1960s.

Sammy Solway took this view a little further down the road, c. 1906. It has been suggested that the small white building on the right contained toilets for the cottages on the other side of the road. The large stone building was a barn, and on the left is Goonbell Chapel. Note the standpipe on the side of the old barn.

Goonbell in 2012 looking towards the old chapel.

The building on the right (above) was at one time a lock-up grocer's shop run by Cereta (Reta) May Thomas and called Lilac Stores. She appears in trade directories in the 1930s, and Barbara Kent remembers her there during the war. Barbara said, 'She had long ginger hair and flowing clothes. She sold buckets, brooms, tea, candles, pinnies, vests etc.'

The lane up on the right just past the old shop is known as 'Meeting House Lane'. A little way up the lane on the right there was a small Wesleyan Methodist chapel. This is shown on the 1880 and 1907 Ordnance Survey maps and was probably in use during that period. Little is known about this chapel, but Donald Blight remembers the foundation stones and other remains, and confirmed that it appeared to have been a small building.

Next to the lane are the ruins of the barn, and beyond this is a shed/garage that was built before the war by Jimmy Thomas as a store for his greengrocery round which covered the St Agnes area. His brother Arthur was also a greengrocer with a store at Goonlaze, and he delivered to the Perranporth area. After the war Jimmy gave up his round and moved to Hurlingburrow Farm, and Arthur took over his store and delivery round in the St Agnes and Mithian areas. Arthur's son Ernest helped his father and said they used a horse-drawn wagon as well as a van to deliver vegetables. He drove one and his father the other.

In December 1962 Arthur gave up the round to farm at Goonlaze, and his brother Raphael took on the business. Raphael bought his own horse and used Arthur's old wagon for his round. Raphael however did not use this building as his store. Many will remember him delivering with his horse and wagon at all hours of the day and night.

Arthur Thomas' horse and delivery wagon in 1957. His brother Raphael later used this wagon on his greengrocery round.

GOONBELL CHAPEL

As with Goonown Chapel, there is some doubt about the exact date when this little chapel was built.

The Goonbell Society, which followed the Primitive Methodist persuasion, was formed in 1846, but by 1848 it was agreed that the Society should cease due to lack of support. Four years later, in 1852, it was reformed, and this time it went from strength to strength.

In his notes held at the Courtney Library, Truro, the Methodist historian Thomas Shaw writes:

> Between 1846 and 1848 a Primitive Methodist Society was formed at Goonbell and in 1852 the mission led to the opening of a chapel. On the 3rd January 1855 at a Redruth Primitive Methodist Chapel it was proposed that two or three dozen old bibles and testaments be given to Goonbell School. (This would support the statement that the Chapel was built between 1852 and 1855.) In 1858 St Day Primitive Methodist circuit accounts contain the item 'Goonbell 30 members. Money turned in £1, 11, 3d [about £1.56].' In the statistical returns of 1973 it states it was opened in 1859.

Shaw concludes:

> If the date given on the statistical return is correct it would appear that the present building was erected in 1859 and succeeded one built a few years before. Taking all evidence given above however it seems possible that the statistical return is incorrect and that the present building was erected between 1852 and 1859.

Goonbell Chapel with the new Sunday School on the right, c. 1960.

In the book *Friendly Retreat* (1955) we read: 'That great little man, Billy Bray, is said to have preached at Goonbell. Mr. A. Kneebone, of Goonbell, recalls that his mother could remember Billy Bray coming there, remarking as he entered the Chapel: "I'm the King's Son" – a title he loved to use.' Billy Bray died on the 25th May 1868, so his visit was during the early years of the chapel.

Frank Carpenter's notes indicate that in 1873 a Manor Court was held at the White Hart, Churchtown, St Agnes, when a lease was granted at a rent of one shilling (5p) a year. In 1884 an attempt was made to purchase a piece of land to build a new chapel, but unfortunately the necessary money could not be raised and the idea fell through. It was then agreed to carry out considerable alterations to the existing building. After this refurbishment the chapel was reopened for services on the 11th January 1885. The alterations were paid for by several fund-raising events, including a service of songs and a bazaar.

More repairs were carried out in 1919 and the *Royal Cornwall Gazette* of the 17th September carried the following report: 'After undergoing thorough renovation, Goonbell Primitive Chapel was re-opened on Saturday, the pastor, the Rev. J. Walker preaching in the afternoon. At the evening meeting addresses were given by the rev. gentleman and Messrs. J. Eva, W. Richards and F. Hunt. The preacher on the Sunday was the Rev. J. Walker.'

Ruth Pearce from Water Lane attended the Sunday School here in the late 1920s: 'I went to Goonbell for a time, then it closed down and I went to St Agnes. They had Tea Treats but I don't think we had a procession; most children went to St Agnes and it was only a small group that lived around the Goonbell area. I remember Victor Trezise being one of the School Superintendents.'

On the 17th July 1929 the *Royal Cornwall Gazette*, under the heading 'Sunday School Festival', carried the following report:

> In connection with the Goonbell Sunday School the annual tea was held on Saturday, when the teachers and scholars headed by St Agnes Town Band, paraded the village and marched to a field at Goonbell, where every child received tea. Tea tables were in charge of the teachers and adults. Sports were arranged and the band gave interesting interludes. On Sunday the anniversary was held. In the afternoon the scholars of the Sunday School gave a musical programme, consisting of choruses, solos, recitations, etc. Musical items were also rendered at the evening service. Mr. W. Bishop of Redruth, presided and Alfred Treglown was accompanist.

Phyllis Robinson (née Spring) attended the Sunday School for three or four years in the early 1930s. She remembered Mary Ann Barkle and Hazel Lawry as teachers.

After the Second World War the congregation declined to such an extent that the chapel was forced to close, but it opened again on the 24th May 1952. Colin and Phyllis Butson attended the Sunday School in the early 1950s and remember Roy Blewett and Ruth Pearce as teachers. The annual treat was a trip to Carbis Bay.

On the 16th January 1955 the chapel was severely damaged by a storm and floods. The end wall collapsed from roof level to within a few feet of the ground. Ruth Pearce remembered this incident well: 'I started as a Sunday School teacher in 1953 shortly after it reopened again. Prior to this there hadn't been a School for a long time. One Sunday morning I was going to the Sunday School and when I got over by Ropewalk Farm I thought, "Whatever is the Chapel looking like?" – it was 10 o'clock in the morning – I couldn't make it out, then I saw the roof down.'

It was thought at first that this might have been the end of this little chapel. The local Methodists, however, decided that this happening should be turned to good effect. The trustees agreed that the chapel should be restored and a much needed school-room added. Ruth Pearce said, 'David White wanted to close it but the Rev. Clapp from Perranporth, his wife and daughter Heather worked hard to keep it open.'

The work was carried out by local builder Albert Reynolds at a cost in the region of £1900. Ruth Pearce said, 'Guthrie Thomas from Trevellas had a window put in the back of the chapel; he gave it to us as a gift. There was nothing there before and it was put in by Albert Reynolds when it was rebuilt.' While repairs to the chapel were being carried out, the congregation went to the old Goonown Chapel to worship.

On the 8th August 1956 the chapel was reopened and dedicated. Twelve months later, on Saturday the 27th July 1957, at 3 p.m., the new school-room was officially opened by Mrs Walter Foxon. At 3.15 p.m. the Rev. Walter Foxon preached at the dedication service.

Ruth Pearce continued to teach there and said, 'In the 1960s we had 25 to 30 children in the Sunday School.'

Unfortunately, as with many small chapels in the area, the number of those attending started to decline, and Ruth remembered congregations as low as four at times. She said, 'Sometimes we never had a pianist, sometimes we did. We managed for a long time hoping that more would turn up, but of course they didn't.'

In 1983 the small chapel closed for the last time, and in 1985 it was converted into a dwelling.

The collapsed end wall of the chapel on the 16th January 1955.

The reopening and dedication of the repaired chapel on the 8th August 1956. (L to R): Rev. Ambrose Payne, Rev. Herbert Crocker, unknown, Rev. F. Sims Clapp and Albert Reynolds. Photo Ken Young.

The inside of the chapel after reopening, showing the stained glass window: a gift from Guthrie Thomas of Trevellas.

The building of the new Sunday School extension in March 1957.

The opening of the new Sunday School building by Mrs Foxon, on the 27th July 1957. Photo Ken Young.

Goonbell Rangers 1906-07

GOONBELL FOOTBALL CLUB

The earliest reference to a Goonbell football team is a postcard showing a team with 'Goonbell Rangers 1906-07' on the ball in front. The team appears to consist of teenage boys and includes a young Reg Trezise, the captain, with the ball between his legs. The writer has been unable to find any reference to this team in any newspaper.

The *West Briton* of the 27th October 1913, under the heading 'Club for Goonbell', wrote:

An Association football club has been formed at Goonbell with the following officers:- President, Mr James Tregea, Treasurer, Mr T. Kneebone, Secretary, Mr W. Kellow, Captain, Mr Percy Solomon and vice-captain Mr George Richards.

Their first match was played, at the beginning of November, on the Goonlaze ground against an eleven from the Perranporth District. Goonbell won 4-2. Later in the month they lost 2-0 to Perranporth. Their first away game was at Truro in December against Truro Rovers and they drew 1-1. In January 1914 they lost 2-0 away to a Bridge XI.

The *Cornish Post and Mining News* of the 28th May 1914 reported a large attendance at the club's annual meeting, but sadly with the coming of the First World War all competition football in Cornwall ceased. The Goonbell club, which had been going for only one season, disbanded.

It would appear that the team reformed for a while after the War. Although very little is recorded, the *Royal Cornwall Gazette* of the 5th May 1920 reported: 'St Agnes Rangers on Saturday entertained Goonbell and won by three goals to nil through Nankivell, Wilford [sic] and Nitchell [sic].' Goonbell are not shown in any leagues at this time and it seems likely that this was just a friendly game.

Goonbell A.F.C. players and committee 1913/14. The writer has been unable to establish which cup is in front of the team.
Back row (L to R): W. Kellow (Secretary), P. Solomon, A. Lobb, F. Barkle, unknown.
Middle row (L to R): unknown, Barkle, E. Pheby, G. Richards, unknown.
Front row (L to R): R. Trezise, J. Barkle, Barkle, F. James, F. Barkle.

SEASON 1947/48

The next reference to a Goonbell team in the newspapers comes in December 1947 when they lost 3-1 away to Mount Hawke, and it seems possible that they were only playing friendly matches in this first season. In March they beat Dolcoath Tech. reserves 4-2 in a friendly.

SEASON 1948/49

This season Goonbell would play in the Cornwall Junior Cup and the Truro and District League. In September they lost 2-0 to Mount Hawke and in October 4-1 away to Perranporth, 6-3 at home to Mithian and 5-0 away to St Erme. At the end of November they were next to bottom of the nine teams in the Cornwall Junior Cup, group B. By January they were bottom of the league despite winning three games. They had played 15, won 3 and lost 12. The season continued with defeats in the Truro and District League including 10-1 away to Perranwell and 7-0 at home to the Truro B. L. At the end of April they were bottom of the league without a win, having played 10 and lost 10.

SEASON 1949/50

Goonbell would play this season in the Junior Cup and the Dunn Cup. In September they lost to Mithian 2-0 but the following week beat Goonhavern 1-0. A 4-3 home defeat by Mount Hawke was then followed by a 5-1 defeat by Zelah. In November they lost 3-2 to a poor St Agnes side and 7-1 to R.N.A.S. Culdrose. In January they lost 5-1 to Zelah and 15-0 away to Truro G.P.O. By the end of January they were next to bottom in the Junior Cup, group B, final placing, having played 12, won 2, drawn 1 and lost 9. They were however above St Agnes who were bottom. In the Dunn Cup more defeats followed, including 8-0 to Truro G.P.O. and 6-1 to Chacewater in March, and they finished bottom of the eight teams in this league.

At the end of the season, Mr C.T.R. Eva, the St Agnes Hon. Sec., wrote to Goonbell and asked them to join the St Agnes club. At the annual meeting of St Agnes football club held in June, Mr Eva read the reply sent by Mr T. Cortis, Hon. Sec. of the Goonbell club. It said that Goonbell would be running a side next season and, from past experience, he did not think that any one junior club could successfully run first and second teams.

Goonbell Football Club in March 1950.
Back row (L to R): Mr Albury, Donald Blight, E. Watson, Tommy Cortis, Archie Pheby, Arthur Thomas, Jimmy Olds and William Cortis.
Front row (L to R): Alan Repper, R. Pearce, J. Migdal, George Wills and Raphael Thomas.

SEASON 1950/51

The season started with a string of heavy defeats including 4-1 to Zelah, 6-2 to Mount Hawke and 11-2 and 8-0 to St Agnes, and by mid-November they were bottom of seven teams in the Junior Cup, group B, having lost all six of their games played. The *West Briton* of the 23rd November, under the heading 'Goonbell withdraw from Junior Cup', reported: 'Because of their difficulty in raising a team Goonbell A.F.C. have withdrawn from the Junior Cup competition. They played in group B.' This was the end of Goonbell football club.

ROPEWALK

From Goonbell to the B3285 St Agnes to Perranporth Road is a stretch of highway called Ropewalk. This is so called because of an occupation that once took place in the area, rope-making. A ropewalk can be described as 'a long building or piece of ground where ropes are made'. Here strands of material, such as hemp fibre, were laid and twisted into rope. It would appear that these rope-making premises were situated where Ropewalk Farm is today. On the 1841 tithe map a property on this site is occupied by William Ferris, although there is no mention of Ropewalk or rope-makers, just a homestead with arable fields. On the 1841 census William Ferris is shown as living at Rope House, aged 40 and a rope-maker. The Rope House entry appears in the census between Goonlaze and Goonbell, and with the house name already in existence it seems likely that rope-making had existed before this date. By the 1851 census William is shown living at Goonown with his wife Mary and three children aged 5, 3 and 2. His occupation is a 'rope maker' employing 2 boys. By the 1861 census he is again living at Goonbell with his occupation now given as a 'master rope maker'. He lived there with his wife Mary and four children, two of whom, William J. aged 15 and James aged 13, are also recorded as rope-makers, suggesting that he is now employing his own sons. In 1871 William is not shown on the census, just Mary and another son, Stephen. In June 1871 the *Royal Cornwall Gazette* advertised the sale by public auction of the 'Rope Walk [sic] with the houses thereon'. The advert said it was situated near Goonbell and occupied by Mrs Mary Ferris. The purchaser also had the option of buying all the machinery on the premises including a small steam engine. It would appear however that the purchaser did not want the machinery, as in December the same year another advert appeared in the newspaper for the sale of rope-making materials, headed 'TO ROPERS AND OTHERS'. The sale included 'an 8-inch cylinder engine, wood beam, 20-inch stroke, with two boilers about a ton, and fly wheel, spinning wheels and jacks, travelling jacks and sleds, patent wheel, bobbins, patent tube and plates, heavy and light hooks, winks, swivels, hatchels, tar capstan, tar furnaces, several sets of tails, old junk, barrel rosin, scales and weights, old iron, blocks, smiths' bellows, vice, anvil, pair mill stones, corn mill, thrashing-machine, old timber, spring cart, nearly new, and miscellaneous effects'. To view, people were again asked to contact Mrs Ferris the owner. This was the end of rope-making in St Agnes.

An aerial view of Goonbell, Ropewalk and Ropewalk Farm c. 1985. The lane leaving Ropewalk, on the bend, and passing under the old railway embankment was an old parish road and can be seen on the 1810 map on page 77.

GOONBELL HALT

G oonbell Halt was opened in August 1905 on the Chacewater to Newquay branch line. The line itself was opened as far as Perranporth in 1903 and from Perranporth to Newquay on the 2nd January 1905. With the exception of Perranporth Beach Halt, all the halts on the line were opened in August of that year.

c. 1950: Goonbell Halt, a traditional Great Western Railway halt with name board, two oil lamps and pagoda-style shelter.

The residents of St Agnes must have been quite disappointed when their station was built nearly a mile from the village centre. Many got off the train at Goonbell Halt, about a quarter of a mile from the station, and walked to the village. Goonbell residents were delighted to have the halt on their doorstep. Barbara Kent said, 'You could tell the time by the trains.' She didn't however appreciate the halt being quite so close to St Agnes Station. She remembered as a young child going to Truro on Saturdays with her mother and often having to walk to the station because the journey was a penny or two cheaper than catching the train at Goonbell Halt.

The branch line closed on the 4th February 1963 and for many years the cutting became a dumping ground. Arthur Robinson, whose house is near the halt, remembers a lot of large black rats in the cutting. He and his son Peter would shoot them with air rifles from the top of the embankment. Later a local haulage company was given permission to dump rubble here and gradually the cutting was filled in to field level.

The only reminders now are one of the bridge parapets and the badly rusted gates by the road.

The derelict rat-infested cutting and shelter in the 1970s.

Goonbell in 2008. The road to Wheal Butson is in the centre of the view, and to the left are the remaining bridge parapet and the rusted gates that led to the halt in the cutting below.

REFERENCES

St Agnes Official Guide, 1925

St Agnes Parish Church Magazines

Chronological History of the People called Methodists by W. Myles

Royal Cornwall Gazette newspapers (Courtney Library, R.I.C., Truro)

West Briton newspapers (Cornwall Centre, Redruth)

Cornish Post and Mining News newspapers (Cornwall Centre, Redruth)

Cornubian and Redruth Times newspapers (Cornwall Centre, Redruth)

Goonown Chapel Trust Account Book of 1838

Kelly's and other trade directories (Cornwall Centre, Redruth)

Friendly Retreat by Maurice Bizley

Maurice Bizley notes (Courtney Library, R.I.C., Truro)

The Lawrences of Cornwall by Edith J. Durning-Lawrence

A Popular Dictionary of Cornish Place-Names by Oliver Padel

Place-Names of Cornwall by J.E.B. Gover

St Agnes Police Occurrence Books (County Record Office, Truro)

A History of Trevaunance Lodge of Free and Accepted Masons No. 4668, 1925-1975

The Journal of the St Agnes Museum Trust:

    No. 2. Some Cornish Place-Names in St Agnes Parish by P.W. Thomas

    No. 7. The Journal of John Carter (1835-1907) edited by Frank Carpenter

    No. 16. St Agnes Feast about 1934 to 1936 by Margaret Davey

Books by the same author:

St Agnes Parish 1850 - 1920: a Photographic Record (1986)

St Agnes Parish 1920 - 1950: a Photographic Record (1988)

Around St Agnes – The Archive Photographs series (1996)

St Agnes: a Photographic History. Volume One – Down Quay (2005)

St Agnes: a Photographic History. Volume Two – Village & Shops (2006)

St Agnes: a Photographic History. Volume Three – Down to Dirty Pool (2009)

Books by the same author with Tony Mansell:

A History of Blackwater and its Neighbours (2004)

Jericho to Cligga, Trevellas and Crosscoombe (2006)

Our Village Church, St Agnes, Cornwall (2007)

Memories of Mount Hawke (2008)

I rode to St Agnes: John Wesley and Methodism in a Cornish Parish (2010)

ACKNOWLEDGEMENTS

This is the fourth book in the Photographic History series and I must thank everyone who has helped me. People again have welcomed me into their homes for a chat over a cup of tea and a piece of cake or answered a small query over the phone. Others have lent me family photographs to scan and use in the book

Among them are: Jane Adams, Donald Blight, Colin Butson, Margaret Davey, Sally Fowler, Alan Green, Olive Keast, Barbara Kent, Douglas Mitchell, Ruth Pearce, Elizabeth Pugsley, Irene Richards (née Roberts), Joe Ridholls, Frank and Pam Roberts, Phyllis and Arthur Robinson, Richie Sandercock, Pam Saunby, Irene Scoble, Stephen Snell, Ernest Thomas, Janet Thomas, Austin Tremain, Jeanette Trezise, Margaret and Ken White.

I have made every attempt to trace individual photographers, and wherever possible I have given them credit for using their images. I apologise to those whom I have been unable to find.

My research has been greatly helped by the excellent staff of the Courtney Library at the Royal Institution of Cornwall, the Cornwall Centre and the County Record Office; these are invaluable sources of information for local historians.

Finally I would again like to thank Peter ('Nick') Thomas for his time proofreading the completed book and my son Daniel for his design and typesetting skills.